MarriageToday

PO Box 59888

Dallas, TX 75229

1-800-868-8349

Ordering Information:

For sales details, contact the publisher at the address above.

Printed in the United States of America

Blending Families

Interactive Workbook for Couples or Groups

Jimmy Evans and Frank Martin

How to Use This Study

Welcome to *Blending Families*, an interactive study guide for couples or groups. If you are in a blended family, or considering marriage with children already in the picture, then you've come to the right place. This study was designed specifically with you in mind!

To get the most out of this study, we encourage you to use it as a companion to our book, *Blending Families*. Many of the ideas and principles we address here are developed in more detail in the book, so if you take time to read that first, you'll be further ahead of the game. It's not a prerequisite, but a good suggestion. We've designed this workbook to be used as a stand-alone study, so whether you are going through it as a couple, or in a small group setting, you should have all you need for an engaging and in-depth study.

Jimmy Evans and the *MarriageToday* team have developed eight videos designed to be used with each session in this workbook. These videos contain candid interviews with many of the eighteen successful stepfamilies we brought together to help with this project. They also contain thoughts and ideas from Jimmy Evans that are not necessarily included in the book or workbook. They will add a great deal to your study, so it's important to watch the corresponding video session for further insight before beginning each week's lesson.

Whether going through this study as a couple, or in a group setting, we encourage you to watch each video to take advantage of this added resource.

Who Will Benefit From This Study?

Simply put, anyone who is either in a blended family, or considering a marriage that will form a blended family, should gain a great deal of wisdom and understanding from this eight-week series. It is designed as a small group resource for blended family support groups, but it can also be used by couples for private study and reflection.

If you have found yourself in a blended family, navigating the unique challenges and dynamics of a stepfamily, then this study was designed specifically with you in mind.

Suggestions for Couples

1) We encourage you to begin each new session in prayer, asking God to give you wisdom as you seek His will for your future.

2) Take time to watch the corresponding video lesson at the beginning of each new session.

3) After reading through the opening thoughts from the week's lesson, don't forget to read the suggested Bible passage. Read it slowly, and meditate on the words before moving on to the lesson. Pray for any specific insight or instruction God may have for you as a couple as you go through the lesson.

4) Write out your answers to each question, just as you would if you were preparing for a group study. It may be tempting to skip over this part and simply meditate on your answers, but writing them out will help you process your thoughts much more clearly. It will also allow this workbook to serve as something of a journal for future reference.

5) End each lesson in final prayer and reflection, asking God to help you incorporate the lessons learned into your daily life. If any particular thought or concept has stood out to you, make a mental note to keep it in your prayers as you go about your day.

Suggestions for Group Study

1) Try to come to each session prepared. You'll get more out of the study if you take time to read through each lesson and answer the questions ahead of time.

2) As you watch the corresponding video lessons, take notes of any thoughts or ideas you'd like to discuss further once the discussion has begun.

3) Come ready to participate. You'll get more out of the lesson if you're willing to involve yourself in the conversation.

4) Try to steer clear of "rabbit trails." In a group discussion, it's often tempting to bring up other situations that come to mind, but that can easily derail the conversation. Try to focus on the question or passage at hand, and it will be much easier for the leader to keep the group on topic.

5)	Listen when others speak, and try not to dominate the conversation. Our personalities often drive how we react during a group discussion, and it's easy for extroverts to unwittingly take over. Try to keep your comments brief and pertinent, and leave room for everyone to participate.

6)	If you are the discussion leader, remember to start on time and end on time. And do your preparation ahead of time, so that everyone in the group can get the most out of each lesson. We've included a "Leader's Guide" at the back of this book to help you do that.

Introduction

Blending Families

When our staff at *Marriage Today* set out to create a comprehensive set of resources for blended families, we wanted to create the most hands-on, realistic, no-nonsense set of tools we could possibly produce. We wanted to give advice that was solid, credible, and proven—and achievable for everyone.

Our goal was twofold:

First, we wanted to give practical, tried-and-true advice on overcoming the inherent "day one" dynamics of a blended family. These are specific challenges that exist at the very beginning of any stepfamily relationship.

Secondly, we wanted to address the special challenges and issues that can happen throughout the changing seasons of life and marriage in a blended family.

Our strategy for accomplishing these goals was to look to those who have already navigated those waters successfully. Experience is always the best coach and mentor, so when trying to blend two families into one, the best place to look for advice is from those who have succeeded in doing just that.

So we began by bringing together eighteen of the most successful blended families we could find. We looked for couples from all walks of life, from different cities and cultures, and at all stages of blended family life. We recruited couples of different ages and backgrounds, each with their own unique sets of challenges and circumstances. Couples who had been through the fire—some several times over—yet come out on the other side intact, healthy, and still going strong. We looked for couples who had succeeded in overcoming the struggles and obstacles that you're likely facing—or will face at some point in the future.

We set out to find healthy and happy blended families who had effectively turned struggles into opportunities for growth. And who welcomed the chance to share what they had learned with others in the same situation.

These couples became our "panel of experts"—the ones that we looked to for workable strategies and advice on growing a strong blended family. And the wealth of wisdom and knowledge they brought to the table surpassed even our greatest expectations. They addressed issues that we didn't even know were issues among today's stepfamilies. And in the end, they helped us create resources for blended families that are far more helpful and insightful than we could have put together on our own.

Defining a Blended Family

So what constitutes a blended family? Let's take some time to define the families and people we had in mind when creating this unique set of resources for stepfamilies.

Like all families, blended marriages come in lots of different shapes and makeups, but the simple definition we've chosen to use is any family unit where one or both parents come into the marriage with a child or children from a previous relationship. The parents may or may not have children with each other, but they come together in marriage with a desire to "blend" their two families.

And these stepfamilies are formed through a number of different scenarios:

1) A husband with children marries a wife with no children.

Sometimes a father with children from a previous relationship will marry a woman with no children of her own. His children are either the result of a previous marriage, a cohabiting relationship, or an extramarital relationship, but they are his responsibility to care for. His new bride may or may not have been married before, but she brings no children into the marriage.

2) A wife with children marries a husband with no children.

Sometimes the previous scenario is reversed. A wife with children from a previous relationship or marriage will marry a husband with no children of his own. He may be divorced or have never been married, but he brings no children of his own into the relationship.

3) A divorced mom with children marries a divorced dad with kids.

This may be the most common scenario among stepfamilies. Two previously married or cohabiting people decide to marry, and each brings a child or children from a previous relationship into the new marriage. It is the typical "Brady Bunch" scenario, where two families come together to make one large family unit. It may feel like the most fun and exciting scenario for a blended family—and it can be. But in reality, it is likely the most challenging stepfamily situation to navigate, since there are lots of different interpersonal dynamics and temperaments involved. In some cases, it can create the "perfect storm" for conflict and friction between siblings and parents.

4) A widow or widower with children remarries.

Some second marriages are formed through the death of a spouse. Either the wife or husband (or both) has children from a previous marriage. Often these kinds of scenarios bring a host of unique struggles and challenges, because there is inevitably a great deal of grief and heartache involved. The loss of a spouse or parent is devastating, and can take years to process. And people grieve in lots of different ways, providing for some special challenges for the family to bond and move forward.

5) Divorced or widowed parents of adult children choose to remarry.

Often stepfamilies are formed after children have already grown and left home. These scenarios may seem like the easiest to navigate, but that's not always the case. Since the children have already left the nest, there is no daily interaction between the families, making it harder for stepchildren to bond with their new stepparent. Instead there may be feelings of jealousy and resentment. It can take years to cultivate a sense of love and intimacy within blended families, and when you don't live under the same roof, those feelings may never have time to develop unless some deliberate steps are taken.

Time to Begin

Obviously, there are other scenarios that bring stepfamilies together, but these are a few of the most common. And these are the situations we had in mind when seeking out our group of successful blended family couples to serve as our panel of experts. The couples we brought together represent a wide range of experiences and circumstances, and are made up of many different types and styles of blended families. They were as diverse as they were insightful. And the collective knowledge, wisdom, and experience they share in the included teaching videos, as well as in the pages to follow are both powerful and practical. We pray that it will change your life, marriage, and family for the better from this day forward.

So stay with us as we set out on this exciting journey toward the healthy—and happy—blended family you always dreamed you could have!

Session One

Beginning to Blend

Trust is the backbone of a marriage relationship. When you have trust, you feel free to experience the full potential of your marriage partnership.

If marriage were a house, trust would be the foundation. It is the cornerstone that anchors and supports the entire framework of the relationship. It is the base upon which all other marital needs and desires are built. And trust is critical to every aspect of a marriage—finances, communication, commitment, faith, accountability, and everything else couples need to survive.

One of the most critical steps to growing a healthy blended family is establishing trust within the relationship—not just between husband and wife, but between children and their new siblings and stepparents.

Learning to Trust Again

"Sometimes I think people are just afraid to put their heart out there and give one hundred percent trust… especially in subsequent marriages," explained Richard. "Because you've been hurt before, and you don't want to get hurt again."

Richard and his wife Sheri had both been married before, and had each experienced a lot of pain and heartache in their previous relationships. They had an intimate understanding of the damage caused when trust is breached, so they committed early in their dating relationship to building a strong foundation of open and honest communication.

"I had some really strong barriers up," confessed Wanda, "It was really hard for me to be open and honest."

Her husband Will had many of the same fears. "We both had baggage coming into this… I was hypersensitive to deceit and manipulation. So I just naturally thought that any person I dated was going to try to control me, or lie to me, or try to deceive me… I had to relearn how to trust."

Couples who have been through a failed relationship almost always come into remarriage with a heightened sense of fear and insecurity, and it takes an extra measure of trust to help them work through it. Any hint of deceit or dishonesty will immediately raise red flags. And deception is the last thing a person needs when trying to trust again.

Helping Children Through the Transition

In a blended family, children also tend to come into the relationship with a heightened level of doubt and insecurity, and often will have many of the same trust issues as their parents. They, too, have likely been wounded by the breakup of their family, and need help overcoming their fears. Kids are seldom equipped to process the emotions they are experiencing, and it takes a special level of sensitivity to help them work through it.

You can succeed as a blended family. You can thrive as a blended family.

"I did a lot of talking and listening," said Renee. "You know, asking them questions about how they felt, what were they thinking. When we actually started planning our wedding, I let them be involved in picking things… making them a part of the whole process."

Kids feel more secure when they know they have a voice, and that their opinion matters. When families make the decision to blend, it has a profound effect on the lives of the children involved. If they feel overlooked or ignored, it will have a marked impact on the success of the blending process.

Children also need to know that the new marriage won't alter or implode their relationship with their other biological parent.

Craig and April brought six children into their marriage, so they knew that they had a special set of challenges to overcome in this area. Craig consistently worked to reassure his kids of his commitment toward them as a father. "I'm still your dad, and I'm going to be your dad no matter what," he told them.

Bonding as a New Stepfamily

Helping children adjust to a new stepfamily is an important step in the process, but it's only the first step. For blended families to succeed, there needs to be a consistent and ongoing emphasis on growing and bonding as a family. The ultimate goal is to create a family unit that no longer feels like "his" children or "her" children, but just another healthy, happy, traditional family.

"As we were married and began blending as a family, we would have a date night every week," explained Renee. "We established game nights where we would have family time. We made sure to schedule family vacations. It was an inclusion process."

Moises and Maggie had many of the same challenges, though it went both ways, since they each brought children into their marriage.

"Coming in as a stepdad," said Moises, "I tried to create memories. I tried to create new memories with the kids. Not to outdate the old memories they had with their dad. But…so that they know I am here to stay, and that we're all in this together."

When helping kids bond into a new blended family, there are no one-size-fits-all set of rules, because all children have different needs and expectations. The key is to understand the struggles your kids may be having, and deal with them on an individual basis. It takes time, patience, and creativity. And it takes an extra measure of love and sensitivity. But with the right attitude and commitment, any blended family can create a safe, happy, and unified environment in the home.

Establishing Right Priorities

"From the classes that I've been through," explained Michael, "I learned personally to put God first, your spouse second, your children third, and your work fourth. I think keeping those priorities in check has really helped me grow as a husband and father."

Keeping right priorities is difficult in any marriage relationship, but especially challenging in a blended family. The inherent "day one" dynamics of a stepfamily create a lot of room for chaos and turmoil, making it hard to keep your focus on what's truly important. But regardless of the challenges, it is critical to the success of your family to keep priorities in proper order. And God's priority is that the marriage always comes before any other human relationship.

"You've now chosen this person as your spouse," she said. "You've made a commitment before God that this is the person you're going to live the rest of your life with. There is a priority that's biblical, and if we don't live by that priority, we're cheating our relationship with our husband. Yes it is our job—and definitely our honor—to raise [our children] up in the way they should go, but they are going to grow and move away. And we still need to maintain and grow our relationship."

> *If a broken marriage hurt your children, a good marriage will heal them.*

In a marriage relationship, anything that comes before your spouse will create tension and resentment. If your career is your highest priority, your spouse will resent your job. If golf or football or baseball is your highest priority, your spouse will feel neglected and jealous of every moment you spend playing and talking about sports. If your children are your highest priority, your spouse will come to resent the time you spend with them, even if they love your kids as much as you do.

The first priority of marriage is that the marriage always has to come first. Only your relationship with God is more important.

Children thrive in an environment of safety and security, and the safest place they can be is in a home with two parents who put each other first, in every circumstance. If it was a broken marriage that hurt your children, it's a healthy marriage that will help them heal. They don't need your constant doting and attention. They need stability. They need a healthy and secure home in which to grow. They need parents who are happy and committed to each other and to the marriage relationship.

Today's Reading:

Proverbs 3:5-6; Psalm 118:8

A Biblical Perspective:

1) How is it comforting to know that you can trust God, even when others have let you down?

2) How does this knowledge help you learn to trust again in your new marriage?

3) How can we learn to regain trust once we have been wounded in a previous relationship?

4) What are some other passages or stories in the Bible that give you comfort when you struggle to trust?

How We Blend:

1) Why is trust so critical to a marriage relationship?

2) Do you agree that trust is the foundation of a healthy marriage and family? Why or why not?

3) Why is trust often so difficult in a blended family?

4) What are some of the more profound trust issues you've experienced because of the breakup of your first marriage or relationship?

5) In what ways are your children or stepchildren struggling with trust issues in your blended family relationships?

6) How do you help your children navigate any difficult emotions they may be having?

7) How are your children accepting the new dynamics of your blended family?

8) What are some concrete things you've done to help your kids bond with their new parent and stepsiblings?

9) Read Ephesians 5:31. Discuss what it takes within a marriage covenant to become "one flesh."

10) Why did God establish marriage as the most important human relationship a person can have?

11) As a group, discuss concrete ways that couples can work to establish trust in a new stepfamily.

12) Why is it especially difficult for stepfamilies to keep right priorities in a new blended family?

13) What would you say is the most critical step to keeping right priorities within a blended family?

14) Have each member of the group give one example of how couples can keep their marriage as their highest human priority.

For Personal Reflection

What would you say is the most insightful point or principle that you learned from this week's lesson? Write your answer in the space below, then share your answer with the group. As a group, spend some time in prayer as you end the session.

Pray specifically for God to guide your thoughts and hearts in the weeks to come as you learn to more effectively blend—both as a family, and a small group.

_____

_____

_____

_____

_____

_____

Between You And God

Heavenly Father, we praise You for being a God in whom we can put unwavering trust. As sinners in a fallen world, we ask for Your grace to cover our failings, and for Your healing and power that enables us to forgive others. Give us wisdom and guidance as we seek to bond together and love each other as a family. May we always try to put You first—committing our way to You, knowing that You will guide our steps.

In Jesus' Name, Amen.

Session Two
Overcoming "Day One" Dynamics

Today, about half of all families are blended families. And they deal with some unique challenges that non-blended families don't have to navigate. Most often there is a history of pain and disappointment. There are likely feelings of guilt, shame, or regret. There are ex-spouses in the picture, and financial obligations already in place. And most often there are precious children caught in the middle of it all, struggling with a lot of the same emotions that their parents are fighting to overcome. The dynamics can feel overwhelming, especially to those who go into the relationship unequipped and unprepared.

The Ghosts of Relationships Past

Not all blended families are products of divorce. Some are formed through the death of a spouse, or a previous extramarital relationship. Sometimes people have children out of wedlock, and other times they decide to take on the responsibility of raising children from a close relative—maybe a grandchild, or a niece or nephew. Some single people decide to adopt, and then later bring those children into a marriage. But statistics show that the majority of stepfamilies are formed through either the dissolution of a marriage, or the breakup of a long-term dating or cohabiting relationship.

Forgiveness doesn't make them right, it just makes you free. Until you let the past go, it will not let your future live.

Anytime a relationship dissolves, you have ghosts of the past to deal with. And these ghosts can haunt you in ways you might never have expected.

Unresolved Anger and Resentment

Divorce is a horrible thing to go through. Any time a relationship ends, there is a wake of damaged feelings and emotions. And that's especially true when the relationship involved sexual intimacy. It's difficult to forgive someone who once held your heart in their hands, only to later reject you.

Anytime we have unresolved anger and resentment toward another person, we risk transferring the offense onto those we love most. And this transference of guilt can happen no matter who it is we're mad at, whether it's an ex-spouse, a previous lover, a former business partner, or even a friend who wounded us. Wherever unresolved pain resides, there are defense mechanisms in place to keep us from getting hurt again.

And the only way to truly stop the cycle is to resolve the pain once and for all.

Lowered Trust & Higher Expectations

In almost every remarriage there are two very real "day one" dynamics that couples have to overcome.

The first is a lowered level of trust. People who have been through a divorce on the heels of a bad marriage are normally going to feel less trustful when it comes to relationships. They've been wounded before, and they don't want to be wounded again.

The second is a higher level of expectation. People who have been hurt in the past tend to be more cynical, sensitive, and suspicious. Their last partner failed to live up to their expectations, and somewhere deep in their spirit they expect their new partner to fail them as well.

Lowered trust and higher expectations is the ultimate "one-two" combination. It's not only unfair; it creates a standard that's virtually impossible to attain, and can easily implode a marriage if not dealt with in a healthy manner.

Unhealthy Inner Vows

Inner vows are promises we make to ourselves in times of difficulty, turmoil, or pain. And they can easily become the force that guides our lives and actions when we become adults. Any area in which we feel betrayed, mistreated, or powerless creates within us the potential for a dangerous and unhealthy inner vow.

And wherever we have an inner vow, we become irrational and un-teachable. Our actions may feel perfectly reasonable, but they don't make sense to anyone but us.

And we all have them. I've never known a person to reach adulthood without having some form of inner vow somewhere within them. We've all been wounded, and because of it, we've all made promises to ourselves in order to keep from getting hurt again.

"I'll never let anyone treat me like that again!"

"No one will ever speak to my kids that way again!"

"I'll never allow anyone to cheat on me, or lie to my face the way he did!"

On the heels of pain and heartache, these dangerous inner vows set up shop in our hearts and falsely promise to guard our hearts from ever getting hurt again.

But they also become one of the greatest hurdles we have to building intimacy within marriage. In a blended family, inner vows must be recognized and broken in order to experience true happiness and intimacy.

Yours, Mine, or Ours?

In a traditional first marriage, husbands and wives come into the relationship with no children, and the entire focus of the marriage is on each other.

But in blended families, things aren't always that easy. In blended families, you have children, and then you try to introduce a marriage into the mix. The relationships between parents and children are already established, and then suddenly there is a new parent in the house. It's common for kids to feel a little jealous or apprehensive.

Kids who have lost a father to divorce don't always want a new father. In their minds, they already have one. They're just upset that he doesn't live with them anymore.

Kids who have been separated from their biological mother, whether it was through divorce or death, have lost a deeply integral part of their lives. They will always miss their "real" mother, even if she wasn't the best mother to them.

Most children will instinctively reject anyone who tries to take the place of their biological parent. And when parents enable this natural tendency by taking sides, or not allowing the new stepparent to share the role of parenting, it creates a level of tension and chaos that can quickly compromise the new marriage.

For families to truly "blend," it takes an intentional level of work and effort on the part of everyone involved.

In healthy blended families, children are never seen as his or hers; they are always "ours." And the chain of command should be the same as it is in any traditional family unit.

God created families with a healthy sense of hierarchy, and that's the only approach to building a strong family unit. This is true whether the family is a traditional one, or a blended one.

Dealing With an Ex-Spouse

In almost every blended marriage, there are ex-spouses somewhere in the picture. And because children are involved, those ex-spouses will always play a role in the dynamics of your family.

You will probably at some point be tied to them financially, either through shared property, or through alimony payments. You will be tied to them physically, because of their shared interest in your children. You will be tied to them emotionally, because they will always want to have some say in how the children are raised. And you will be tied to them spiritually, because they have open communication with your children, and are able to pass on values and ideas that you may not always appreciate or agree with.

In many circumstances, having an ex-spouse in the picture can be a challenge to the marriage, and detrimental to the health of the family unit. Yet it is something that you have to deal with, because when your children have another biological parent in the world, that relationship has to be respected.

Navigating the "Day One" Dynamics

All of these "day one" dynamics are very real issues that blended families have to deal with, and how you handle them will have a marked impact on your ability to truly blend as a family. It takes an extra measure of patience and wisdom to navigate the unique challenges that they bring into your home. But with the right attitude and approach, any family can get through them intact, and go on to be a strong and healthy family unit.

Today's Reading

Mark 10:7-9; Matthew 5:34; Ephesians 4:1-3; Ephesians 4:31-32

A Biblical Perspective

1) Why is it so difficult to feel truly forgiven after the breakup of a marriage?

2) What would God say to someone who is trying to move forward on the heels of divorce or sexual sin?

3) Why are inner vows an offense to God?

How We Blend

1) What are some of the more prominent "day one" dynamics that you've experienced as you've worked to establish a healthy blended family?

2) Do you feel that you have any unresolved anger or resentment issues from your past relationships?

3) In what ways have these issues affected your new marriage and family?

4) Do you sense that your children or stepchildren are struggling with any unresolved anger or resentment issues from their past?

5) How are you helping them navigate any damaging emotions they may be experiencing?

6) Why do you think remarriages bring about higher expectations among couples?

7) Have you found yourself struggling with unrealistic expectations in your new marriage? In what ways?

8) How can you take steps to communicate and manage your expectations of your spouse and children?

9) As a group, discuss some of the more common inner vows that people experience on the heels of divorce.

10) Do you have any unhealthy inner vows from your previous relationships? If so, where do you think they came from? What were the promises you made to yourself through your inner vows?

11) If anyone in your group is struggling to overcome any damaging inner vows, consider taking a few minutes to pray for them as a group.

12) How have you worked to create a sense of unity among your children and stepchildren?

13) If your ex-spouse is still in the picture, how have you worked to keep that dynamic from negatively affecting your new marriage and family?

14) If you could say one thing to your ex-spouse about your expectations from them when it comes to co-parenting, what would it be?

15) Talk about some of the more common types of unresolved anger issues that people experience on the heels of divorce.

16) What are some concrete things you can do as parents to help children overcome their fears and insecurities, and embrace their new family?

For Personal Reflection

In the space below, write out the one most important points or principles you learned from today's lesson, and explain how you plan to apply this to your daily life. Commit to praying this week that God would guide you in this new commitment.

_____

_____

_____

_____

_____

Between You And God

Heavenly Father, we thank You for Your infinite care, love, and faithfulness toward us. We acknowledge You as our provider. Forgive us for trying to take things into our own hands when we establish unhealthy and misguided inner vows. May we release them completely to You, trusting in Your provision as we navigate our relationships. Help us to operate in wisdom and in love. In Jesus' Name, Amen.

❖   *In this teaching Jimmy Evans introduced the concept of having a vision retreat with your spouse. A vision retreat is the best way for you and your spouse to come into agreement for every area of your marriage for the upcoming year. The process of having a vision retreat will be discussed in more detail during Session 6.*

Session Three
Dealing With Damaged Emotions

All marriages have to deal with pain and baggage from past hurts and relationships. We are flawed and sinful people, and we live in a fallen world. Even young couples entering into marriage for the first time are going to experience turmoil because of past wounds and damaged emotions.

But blended families usually have an even greater degree of stress and tension to deal with. By their very nature, remarriages are riddled with much more baggage from past relationships, and wounds that are likely deeper and more pronounced.

Dealing With Past Pain

"As the new spouse in a blended family," said Charles, "I think it's important that you understand your role from day one. And a part of your role will be—not may be, but will be—to help them heal. To establish new trust, new belief, now hope in relationships. And to help them process in a really gracious and understanding way."

Patience and acceptance are important in any new marriage, but especially critical when you know your spouse is struggling with past wounds and insecurities. It takes a special measure of love and commitment to bring healing to a damaged heart. And that's something you can give your spouse that they can't get from any other human relationship.

And wherever there is pain, there is bound to be conflict. Learning to navigate conflict is an important part of living in a blended family.

"You can't be afraid of conflict," said Sheri. "Without conflict there is no growth. And blended families are going to have conflict. You're going to have trial and error. You're going to get back up, dust yourself off, and you're going to be great, and then you're going to fall again. You just can't give up, because things are going to get better."

Past pain does more than create conflict. It also causes inner turmoil and self-hate. People who come into marriage with regret often have trouble forgiving themselves. And it's almost impossible to move forward until you truly put your past behind you.

Making Peace With the Past

"One of the major ways I've been able to heal from the past," said April, "is I've really had to realize that my husband is not my ex-husband. Sometimes [I would] deal with situations in the same manner because of those past hurts."

It's not about your past, it's about your future.

Like many remarried spouses, April had found herself transferring her anger toward her ex-husband onto her new husband Craig. And it took a conscious, concerted effort on her part to change that negative pattern of behavior.

Anytime a relationship ends, there are unprocessed wounds residing in the depths of our hearts. And the more emotional ties you have, the longer it may take to get past them. But it's something that needs to be done in order for your new marriage to grow and develop. Not just for your sake, but for the sake of your children.

In a blended family, there is also the temptation to demonize an ex-spouse or a previous partner.

"I also think praying for your ex-spouse is important," said Jesi. "We both have done that… God can change a heart. I think it's important that you pray for them, and you ask God to change their heart. And if you need your heart changed, that you ask God to change your heart if there's anger or hurt or past wounds from that marriage."

Praying for those who have hurt us is one of the most important steps toward healing and forgiveness. It is extremely difficult to harbor a grudge toward someone when you are actively praying blessings over their life and future. It's hard to stay mad at someone while you're asking God to bless them. And it's a critical step in truly moving forward.

Dealing With the Stigma of Remarriage

"I think it's important for us to remember that our identity is not in the fact that we have a blended family," said Jesi. "For us, having a blended family is something that we treasure."

One of the most difficult aspects of living in a blended family is dealing with the stigma attached to divorce. There is still a measure of criticism and disapproval in the body of Christ toward stepfamilies. And even outside the church, there are lots of social stigmas to overcome. Blended families often struggle to feel accepted and appreciated in many circles of society. But it's a stigma that healthy stepfamilies find a way to shake off in order to move forward.

"I would have to say that a blended family is a perfect example of God's redemption," said Renee. "Just like Pastor Jimmy says, 'This could be your eighth marriage, but if you do it God's way, it can be the marriage of your dreams.' It's so true. It doesn't matter what your past is. Blended families are the perfect example of how God can take what was so broken… and blend it perfectly together and make it very beautiful."

Embracing God's love and forgiveness is a critical step toward developing a successful stepfamily, even if you feel judged by others. None of us can undo the past, and God doesn't expect that from us. God looks only to a bright future, and we need to learn to do the same.

Today's Reading:

Mark 11:25; Matthew 6:15; Matthew 18:21-22

A Biblical Perspective:

1) Why is forgiveness so critical in God's economy?

2) What happens to us emotionally and spiritually when we hold a grudge, or choose not to forgive?

3) What do you sense God saying to you through these passages?

How We Blend:

1) In what ways do blended families have more stress and tension to deal with than most first marriages?

2) What are some of the more prominent issues of pain and stress that people experience when they remarry?

3) In what ways has the pain from your past relationships affected your new marriage?

4) What are some of the ways your spouse has helped you navigate the damaging emotions you've experienced?

5) How can parents help their children heal from past wounds and hurts?

6) Read Psalm 34:18. How does this verse bring you comfort when dealing with past pain and disappointment?

7) How do you handle conflict when it arises?

8) In what ways can conflict be a healthy thing in marriage?

9) Transference of blame is common in blended families, but it isn't healthy. What are some of the more common ways we tend to blame our spouse for the transgressions of our exes?

10) Have you found yourself transferring blame onto your spouse from your previous marriage or relationships? If so, how have you worked to change this negative pattern of behavior?

11) Read Philippians 3:13. Why is it so important to make peace with your past in order to move forward in a healthy blended family?

12) What happens when we pray for those who have done us wrong? Why do you think God wants us to do that?

13) In what ways have you felt the stigma of divorce and remarriage?

14) How do you deal with it when sensing that people are judging or criticizing you for your remarriage?

15) Discuss some specific things remarried couples should do in order to overcome the stigma of divorce and remarriage?

16) Have you fully embraced God's love and forgiveness? How does that affect your life and marriage on a daily basis?

God doesn't throw people away, God redeems people. Do not let the scars of your past define your future.

For Personal Reflection

What is the one verse in the Bible that brings you the most peace and comfort during moments of doubt or shame or fear? What do you feel God saying to you through this verse? This week, commit to praying each day for God's comfort and blessing as you reflect on this particular verse.

_____

_____

_____

_____

Between You And God

Heavenly Father, we thank and praise You for being the God of comfort, who comforts us in all of our affliction. We acknowledge our part in the pain of our past relationships, and ask not only for Your forgiveness, but that You would help us to walk victoriously in it. May we also forgive from our hearts those who have wronged us. May we daily press on toward what You would have us to be and to do. In Jesus' Name, Amen.

Session Four

Parenting and Discipline

For blended families to work, parents have to learn to accept stepchildren as their own. And children must respect and obey both parents. A positive stepparent relationship is critical to the success of the family, and essential for a happy, harmonious household.

So how do you connect with your stepchildren as a parent and a friend? How do you learn to love a stepson or stepdaughter the same as your biological children? Is it possible to treat them all the same? And what should parenting and discipline look like in a healthy blended family?

Equal Commitment Versus Equal Love

"Honestly," said Renee, "how can you say that you love [your] stepchild the same as your biological child, when there has been so much more history? It would be hard to say that truthfully. But as far as your commitment to the best interest of that child, you have committed your life to [their] father, and that love and that commitment is going to help you always seek the best interest of that child."

Stepparents often set unrealistic expectations for themselves when it comes to bonding with their stepchildren. They think that they are supposed to have the same feelings for a stepchild as they do toward their biological children, so they tend to overcompensate.

The best approach is to let the process happen naturally. And to let your stepchildren set the pace for the relationship. If you allow them to bond in their own time, and in their own way, the relationship will grow at a healthier pace, and eventually be even stronger.

"It's very difficult to love someone else's child the way that you love your own," confessed Jesi. "It's a different relationship. A mother's love is going to be different. I have committed to be the best parent that I can be to both of my children. And I know that they know that that's my commitment to them."

Avoiding Stepsibling Rivalry

Stepchildren also need to learn to bond with each other. And that, too, may take time and patience. Anytime two families come together under one roof, jealousy and suspicion are bound to arise. Children may not like the idea of sharing their parent with another child, and they will be naturally protective and cautious. It is our job as parents to diffuse any feelings of resentment or distrust.

"If you can spend individual time with each child," said Charles, "I believe it would… help to squash any sibling rivalries, or blended sibling rivalries. I think you also should sit down with both children and allow them to voice their opinions in a respectful way. Sit down and say, 'What do you think about this? How are we doing in this area?'"

The Bible promises when your children mature, they will come back to what you've taught them. You can't produce all immediate results.

As in all human relationships, communication is critical to overcoming sibling rivalry. When children aren't getting along, it's a mistake to remain silent and hope that things will naturally work themselves out. They will usually just get worse. The best approach is to address the problem head-on and help children talk things through. Encourage them to discuss their feelings openly and truthfully, and then help guide them as they work to overcome any relational issues they may be having.

Kids are going to argue and disagree. So it's important not to overreact when they do. But it's also important to recognize ongoing problems of sibling rivalry, and to do whatever it takes to help kids get past it.

Guidelines for Discipline and Correction

"I know how my son feels when I discipline him," says Ty. "He's mad. He doesn't like it. And he loves me. I've been there from the beginning. So imagine how a child is going to feel when a stepparent steps in and tries to administer discipline."

Whether dealing with kids in a traditional family or a blended one, the number one rule is to always show a united front. When kids sense that their parents are not on the same page when it comes to rules and discipline, they can easily capitalize on it, playing one parent against the other.

As a general rule of thumb, new blended families should allow the biological parent to be the primary disciplinarian, but let it be known that both parents have equal authority in the home. And, that they both agree on what is and isn't acceptable behavior.

It's also critical that you not allow your children's other parents to undermine your authority. One of the hardest aspects of sharing custody of your kids with another parent is maintaining consistency and stability when it comes to discipline and instruction.

If at all possible, the best approach is to openly communicate your wishes with your child's other parent. If you have concerns about the way they discipline, find a time to discuss it honestly. If they allow your kids to do things that you don't approve of, calmly talk about it with them, and see if you can come to a mutual compromise.

Dealing With Kids in Crisis

"Whenever you're dealing with a child in crisis in a blended family," advises April, "don't keep it hidden. Reach out. Reach out to a pastor or counselor… definitely do not keep it hidden… because breaking the rules is just a symptom of something deeper. If you're finding that your child is doing drugs, smoking pot, having sex, whatever it is… those are just symptoms to fill a hurt that's in their heart."

When kids go into crisis, parents need to be a united front.

Children often come into blended families with a lot of hidden pain and anger from the past. If they experienced the breakup of their biological family, they are likely still harboring feelings of sadness and resentment.

The best approach in these situations is to begin by spraying yourself with Teflon, and realize that it isn't really you they are mad at. Then deal with the problem head-on. Children who rebel, no matter what their age, need to know that their behavior is unacceptable. That's true in any family, not just a blended one.

A parent's most important role, whether raising a biological child or a stepchild, is to get them to adulthood with their faith intact and their reputation unharmed. And the best way to do that is to stay on your knees, and keep your wits and emotions in check. Pray daily for God to guide their hearts and minds. And for wisdom as you mentor them through times of crisis and turmoil.

Today's Reading

Ephesians 6:4; 1 John 3:16; Philippians 2:2-4; Proverbs 19:18

A Biblical Perspective

1) What do these passages have to say to parents regarding raising children?

2) According to 1 John 3:16, what is real love? How can this give you confidence as you parent your children and stepchildren?

3) Why is it so important to discipline children?

How We Blend

1) For blended families to work, parents have to learn to accept stepchildren as their own. What are some of the best methods to accomplishing this goal?

2) What would you say is the toughest hurdle you have to overcome in parenting a stepchild?

3) What are some things you've done to better connect with your children and stepchildren?

4) Do you think it's possible for parents to love a stepchild as much as they do their biological children? Why or why not.

5) When bonding with a stepchild, the key is time, commitment, and allowing the process to happen organically. How has this worked (or not worked) in your blended family?

6) In what ways have you set unrealistic expectations for yourself when trying to bond with your stepchildren?

7) What are some concrete things you've done to ease yourself and your children into the process of blending as a family?

8) What are some of the biggest mistakes you've made in learning to discipline a new stepchild?

9) How has this lesson changed the way you discipline as a stepparent?

10) Who would you say is the primary disciplinarian in your household? Is it a role you share equally? Explain.

11) In what ways has your ex-spouse unwittingly (or knowingly) undermined your authority as a parent?

12) What are some ways you have been able to alleviate sibling rivalry in your home?

13) Why is a united front so important when parenting children and stepchildren?

14) Do you agree that this is harder to achieve in a stepfamily than in a traditional one? Explain your answer.

15) Have you had to deal with any serious crises among your children or stepchildren? Explain your answer.

16) What is the most important thing to remember when dealing with a child in crisis or rebellion?

17) How can we keep from overreacting when kids rebel? Why is it important not to overreact?

18) In one sentence, what would you say is a parent's most important job when it comes to raising children or stepchildren?

For Personal Reflection

What is the most important point or principle you learned from today's lesson? How do you plan to implement this new principle into your role as a parent? Write your answer below, then commit to praying for God's help in this area during the coming week.

_____

_____

_____

_____

_____

Between You And God

Heavenly Father, we thank You for showing us what real love is, in that Jesus laid down His life for us. We ask for Your grace to do the same with our spouses and our children. May we as husband and wife be of one mind and accord to the extent that our children absorb this mindset every day. Give us the will and wisdom to train up our children in the way they should go, and to believe that You are greater than any crisis that comes our way. In Jesus' Name, Amen.

Session Five

Inter-Relational Issues

Joint custody arrangements can be exhausting, especially after an acrimonious breakup. How do you arrange pick up and drop-off times? Where will kids spend the holidays? What about special occasions, vacations, birthdays, piano recitals, and other important events that involve the children? And how do you go about establishing rules and boundaries that everyone can agree on?

There's nothing about this type of co-parenting that is easy or ideal, but it's a reality that must be dealt with—especially when mandated by the courts. The key is to focus entirely on the needs of the children, and keep their well-being at the center of every conversation and decision. Their desire is to maintain a close relationship with both sets of parents, and that should be both parents' desire as well.

Navigating Joint Custody Issues

"You don't make the child a messenger," said Renee. "You don't send messages to the other parent through the child. If it's not a cordial relationship, write a note or letter, or whatever else you have to do, but I think it's important not to make the children a go-between. Those kinds of things just breed conflict, and more insecurity and fear."

When your relationship with an ex-spouse is strained and tense, it's tempting to let your children communicate for you. This is an easy habit to fall into, and far more convenient than trying to contact them on your own. But it's terribly stressful for the children. They don't want to run screens for parents that can't get along, and we should never allow ourselves to burden them with that responsibility.

Our goal as parents should be to make joint custody as easy on the children as we can. The less stress we create, the better they will adjust to the idea of going back and forth between two families.

Philip and Valenceia had a problem that comes up a lot in shared custody situations. Her ex-husband's wife would call on a moment's notice and ask to pick the kids up early for dinner or a special event. They wanted to be amicable, so they usually agreed. But it created a lot of undue hurry and stress. They would scramble to get things together, and then meet the other parent at a parking lot to pass off the children. It was getting to be a huge problem.

"It would be an inconvenience," Valenceia explained. "Either we would have to meet her, or we'd have to wait for her to come get him, and we never knew how much time that would be."

Their advice to anyone in this situation is to establish clear boundaries with your ex-spouse, and then do whatever it takes to enforce them. When something is creating a problem, don't be afraid to sit down with your ex and talk it through. As always, if you keep the focus on what's best for the child, most reasonable parents will be willing to compromise.

Dealing With Negative Influences

Ex-spouses don't always share our spiritual views and values, and sometimes they undermine our authority by ignoring the rules and guidelines we've set for our children. It's tough to parent with consistency when you have to share custody with a parent who isn't on the same page.

Craig and April had to deal with this dynamic firsthand. They often worried about what their kids might see or experience when they were with their other parent. They had to learn to fight the urge to grill their children, and instead trust God to guide their hearts and eyes.

Have faith that your children are being impressed by you being an example to them. Children are smarter than we sometimes think they are

"People in any relationship want to feel like they have control," explained Craig. "And you don't. You do not have control. What you have are boundaries, guidelines, and love. And you do the best you can."

Renee had good advice for parents in this situation.

"I would just encourage parents who are sending kids into circumstances that may be challenging," advised Renee, "to coat everything in prayer. Lift them up the whole time they're gone, before they go… I think setting the moral standard in your home is key. And anything that you're concerned about, just encourage them in loving ways, without condemning the other parent."

And Philip agreed.

"We have to trust God," said Philip. "At the end of the day, when he's over there it's out of our hands. It's in God's hands."

When Adult Kids Reject Your Relationship

One hurtful dynamic that a lot of blended families have to deal with is adult children who refuse to accept the new relationship, and choose instead to pull away and reject the new spouse. They may still harbor feelings of anger and resentment over the divorce, and don't want to see either of their parents in a new relationship.

"One of the things that I had to deal with a lot was guilt," said Renee, "because I felt like it was my fault that he couldn't have a relationship with his daughter. And it really was hard for me. I felt so guilty… It used to just really eat me up."

Renee's husband Scott struggled deeply when his children refused to accept their new marriage. But he eventually learned to give it to the Lord.

Get in the habit of praying together, especially when something bad is happening. Do not take what is happening as a final verdict.

"My encouragement for anyone who has to choose their spouse over their adult child," said Scott, "is to surrender that to the Lord. That's what we had to do. As hard as that is. We tried everything we could to reconcile that relationship, and to draw them in and include them… If they ultimately are bent on dividing you, you have to choose your spouse and surrender them to the Lord."

In any family, the marriage always has to come before all other human relationships. Even before your children. It's the first priority of marriage, and a principle given to us by God.

If you've found yourself in this situation, in need of redemption and restoration with your adult children, our panel's advice was to hold fast, and always do the right thing. Then trust God to honor your faithfulness and commitment.

God can do a miracle in any heart, no matter how wounded or hardened it may have become.

Today's Reading

Matthew 5:44-45; Matthew 5:9; Nahum 1:7; Exodus 14:13-14

A Biblical Perspective

1) Why is it important to pray for those who have hurt us?

2) What do these passages say about the importance of peace and cooperation when dealing with an ex-spouse?

3) What does Exodus 14:13-14 have to say to us when our kids are in situations that are beyond our control?

How We Blend

1) What are some of the more difficult inter-relational issues that you've had to navigate as a blended family?

2) Talk about ways you have worked to overcome these difficult issues.

3) What are some of the most difficult aspects of joint custody that you've experienced?

4) Why is shared custody so difficult on children?

5) What are some concrete ways we can work to make shared custody easier for children to deal with?

6) What is the best advice you can give someone when they have to share their children with an ex-spouse who is a bad influence on the children?

7) How do you go about negotiating parenting decisions with your ex-spouse?

8) How have you worked to maintain a healthy dialogue with your ex?

9) How do you help make it easier on your kids as they transition from home to home?

10) What is the best approach when an ex-spouse allows your kids to see or do things at their home that you don't allow in your home?

11) How do you talk to your children about this without sounding bitter and controlling?

12) Have you worked to establish healthy boundaries with your ex-spouse? Explain why or why not.

13) What do you worry most about your children when they spend time with their other biological parent?

14) Do you feel that their other biological parent shares your spiritual views and values? Explain why or why not.

15) It's hard on parents when their adult children don't accept their new marriage. Have you experienced this in your family? If so, how have you learned to cope?

16) Before closing, spend time praying for any difficult parenting issues that members of your group might be experiencing.

For Personal Reflection

In the space below, write out your single biggest concern for your children or stepchildren as they navigate the inter-relational issues in your family. How do you think God would have you pray about your concerns? Commit this week to praying about this specific issue on a daily basis.

If you feel comfortable, share it with the group and ask them to pray with you throughout the coming week.

_____

_____

_____

_____

_____

Between You And God

Heavenly Father, we praise and thank You for Your goodness, and for being a stronghold in the day of trouble. The hearts, minds, and souls of our children mean everything to us, and in times of spiritual attack, we confess that we do not always know what to do, but our eyes are on You. We ask for harmonious relationships with all who are in our children's lives, and we thank You for never giving us or our children more than we can bear. In Jesus' Name, Amen.

Session Six
In-Home Blended Family Dynamics

Traditional families have the luxury of starting out together, and getting used to each other as the family grows. They have a long history of navigating issues of personal space, sleeping arrangements, and family rules and traditions. The parents have usually established these things before they had kids, so everyone knows what to expect.

But all of these things become issues when you set out to blend two families into one. You are integrating kids who have never lived together, and parents who likely have different parenting styles and ideas about what family holidays and vacations should look like.

Creating a sense of unity and family identity in this type of environment is often harder than it might appear. It takes a level of intentionality to create a truly "blended" feel within a blended family, and our panel of successful stepfamilies had a lot of great ideas to draw from.

Creating a Sense of Unity

"To create unity and identity for our family," said Renee, "the first thing we did was not to refer to our children as stepchildren, or his children and my children. We tried to always refer to them as 'our' children."

While it may be too early to expect your new stepchildren to call you 'Mom' or 'Dad,' it's never too soon to begin referring to them as your children. Introducing her son as your 'stepson' may be more accurate, but it's a term that may subtly feel like a disclaimer. Especially to kids who are already struggling to accept their new family.

Another important strategy for creating unity is to begin forming family traditions and activities.

"We did family time together," said Renee. "We did game nights. We tried to create things that helped us interact on a friendlier, fun level. I think that's important for kids, especially."

Pete and Shana had a similar suggestion.

"How we created our new family identity," said Pete, "was to sit together as a family, pretty much for every meal—every dinner. And have conversations—open conversations. It created an atmosphere where everyone could share what they were feeling, you know, what their day was like. I think that helps."

Family mealtimes create a prime opportunity to get all of the family together at least once each day to just laugh and talk and enjoy being together. Having dinner in the den in front of the television may sound more relaxing, but it is a wasted opportunity for growth.

Family holidays are also prime opportunities for bonding as a family.

"One of the things my wife stressed," explained Philip, "was, we need to start our own traditions. We need to have our own thing going on at our house so our kids can have memories of that. They can have memories of waking up on Christmas Day and leaving their bedroom and going to the Christmas tree and opening their presents at home."

Strong family traditions create regular times of engagement for the family, and generate a sense of anticipation and excitement. Kids see holidays as something to look forward to, and a time to just enjoy being together and to have fun as a family.

Developing Personal Space

"In regard to personal space," confessed Charles, "when we first got married, it didn't go over so well. I immediately came in as the non-biological parent and established my domain. He [Ty's son] was used to it being his domain, and it caused a problem between us that affected the whole atmosphere of the house."

Like a lot of new blended families, Charles and Ty had to learn how to integrate more gradually and deliberately. Though Ty's son was young, he still needed to feel that his personal space and standing in the home was respected. It isn't easy having a new dad come into the house and begin to take charge. So Charles learned from his mistakes and began respecting his stepson's personal space.

> *Imagine every year writing down what you believe God's will is for each one of your children and that you are committed to doing that.*

In some blended families, there is also a matter of modesty that needs to be acknowledged and addressed. When stepsiblings of different genders move into the same household, creating clear boundaries and rules of personal space becomes even more critical. This is especially true as children grow older and enter the teenage years.

"We have boys and we have girls,' said Velory, "so we did have to establish some boundaries there."

In most cases, this means establishing clear rules regarding appropriate dress and conduct. Children need to learn to keep doors closed when dressing and undressing, and to knock before entering another sibling's bedroom. Parents should also adhere to more stringent rules of modesty.

Living in harmony takes a lot of patience and communication, especially when trying to blend two previously independent families into one. There are no issues of space and privacy that can't be overcome with the right attitude of caring and cooperation.

Shifting Authority to the Stepparent

When first starting out as a blended family, it's a good idea to let the biological parent be the primary disciplinarian of the children. This gives the stepparent time to relax and get to know his new kids on a more personal and friendly level. This is the approach that most successful stepfamilies took at the beginning, because it works.

But there comes a point when the stepparent's role should begin to shift and take hold, because homes only work when both parents share equal authority over the children. Otherwise the kids will begin seeing the stepparent as passive and disengaged.

As Valenceia explained: "As a stepparent, you have to be consistent, because if you're not, they're not going to take you seriously, or give you that respect, because you're not taking yourself seriously. So you have to [show] a united front—when your spouse is there and when they're not there—you have to be consistent."

Households only run smoothly when both parents are unified in matters of discipline and house rules and expectations. And, when both parents share an equal role in establishing and administering those rules. That's true in every home, not just a blended one. Healthy rules make for healthy families.

When You Have Different Parenting Styles

"It's probably rare that blended family parenting styles, coming together, are going to match," J.D. explained. "So it needs to be a compromise instead of the parents butting heads and the children trying to play them against one another. You have to be on the same page."

Different parenting styles are inevitable any time you have a new blended family. The way we parent is usually established early in our marriages, so we are likely to have more in common with our first spouse when it comes to setting rules and doling out discipline. In second or third marriages, you have to rethink and reestablish those styles. When parenting styles don't match, kids will soon become confused and frustrated. They need to see a unified front, and it's our job to come together in order to find that unity.

In addition to parents with different parenting styles, you also have children with different disciplining needs. It's important to find common ground on how to deal with that as well.

So what happens when you disagree on how best to discipline?

"It's important to pray about it," said Bryan. "Pray together or pray separately before you have some of these conversations. You have to look at it from a respectful perspective."

Parents who pray together over family issues are always going to be better prepared to make wise decisions. And they will be in a better state of mind when they do so.

If you can't solve a problem on your own related to your children, get help. Getting help is not a sign of weakness it is a sign of wisdom.

Today's Reading

1 John 4:7; Ephesians 5:21; Ephesians 6:1-4; 1 Peter 3:8

A Biblical Perspective

1) What do these passages say about the importance of unity and oneness within a family unit?

2) Why is unity so important to God's plan for a family?

3) What would God say to husbands and wives who struggle to be unified in their decisions?

How We Blend

1) What are some of the most common mistakes parents make when trying to blend two families into one?

2) Discuss some of the best ways you've found of helping your stepchildren accept their new reality within your blended family.

3) In what ways have you worked to establish a strong sense of unity and family identity within your blended family?

4) Do you agree that it's important to refer to both children and stepchildren as "our children?" Why or why not?

5) What are some unique family traditions and activities you've developed in your blended family?

6) Why do you think strong family traditions are so important to creating a sense of unity among children?

7) Why is it important to involve children when planning vacations or family traditions? How does that help foster a sense of unity?

8) What are your rules and expectations regarding meal times and family gatherings?

9) What are your thoughts on the idea of an annual vision retreat? What aspects of a vision retreat sound appealing to you? What aspects sound unappealing?

10) Having a vision for your relationship begins by just discussing what you hope to accomplish in the next ten, twenty or thirty years in your marriage? List and discuss your ideas with each other.

_____

_____

_____

_____

_____

_____

11) Look over your answers in the previous question. Summarize what you believe is God's greater purpose for putting you and your spouse together. (Remember God's purposes are always ultimately about relationships.)

_____

_____

_____

_____

12) If you were to go on a vision retreat to renew your marriage and talk about your relationship, when are possibilities that you could go? Where might you go? How many days could you be away? If possible, set a date and begin making plans.

13) What are some of the more difficult issues of personal space you've had to overcome? How did you overcome them?

14) Do you agree that it's a good idea for the biological parent to be the primary disciplinarian of his or her biological children as a family first begins to blend? Why or why not?

15) When do you feel it is appropriate for a new stepparent to begin correcting and disciplining their new stepchildren?

16) What is the best strategy for allowing that shift in authority to happen?

17) When stepparents have different parenting styles and philosophies, what's the best approach to working through those differences?

For Personal Reflection

What is the most important point or principle you learned from today's lesson? How do you think this will change the way you parent in the future? Ask God to guide you as you implement this new strategy or commitment with your family over the coming weeks.

_____

_____

_____

Between You And God

Heavenly Father, thank You for allowing us a glimpse of the unity of the Father, Son, and Holy Spirit. We confess that we have often insisted on our own way, instead of seeking Your will and the good of others. Give us eyes to see how You would have us love those around us, and help us be like-minded, gentle, and humble as we continue to meld our lives together. In Jesus' Name, Amen.

❖ If you'd like more information on how to have a vision retreat, visit MarriageToday.com for the MarriageToday resource, *The Mountaintop of Marriage*. In this guidebook, Jimmy and Karen will walk you step-by-step through having a retreat and developing a vision that will revolutionize your marriage.

Session Seven
Extended Family Relationships

No matter how hard you work at creating peace and harmony within your own four walls, there are relationships outside your walls that have to be navigated just as carefully. In a blended family, you likely have a number of extended family members who want to play a part in your children's lives, and many of them deserve to do so.

Your ex-spouse wants to have some sort of relationship with the children you had together. And your ex-in-laws often feel the same way. They still love and care for their grandkids, and are often struggling to figure out how they factor into your children's future.

Sometimes these relationships are healthy and good for your children. Sometimes they are not. In some cases, you feel the need to protect your kids from people who may harm them emotionally or spiritually.

It's a fine line that virtually every couple in a blended family has to deal with. And no two cases are the same. As parents, it's our job to understand all the dynamics at work in our particular family, and decide how to best handle all the outside factors and influences at work within our extended family relationships.

Dealing With Ex-In-Laws

"We've had grandparents show up on Christmas Day unannounced with gifts… not calling, and just creating a ruckus," explained Ty. "So we really had to set boundaries."

Dealing with ex-in-laws may be one of the more common—and difficult—family dynamics facing most stepfamilies. Your spouse's parents didn't divorce you or your children, but at times they may feel like it. They are usually walking on the same eggshells as you, and don't always handle it as tactfully or sensitively as you might hope. But they are usually doing the best they can in an awkward situation.

When setting boundaries with ex-in-laws, or other extended family members, the focus should always be on what's best for the children. If their relationship with their grandparents is a healthy one—spiritually and emotionally—you likely want them to play a significant role in your children's future. But if it's not, your job is to protect your kids from undue harm.

The best approach is always to be honest, but sensitive. To let your wishes be known, but also be willing to bend and be flexible. Your kids will benefit by getting to know their extended family members, and life will be less stressful if you don't feel the need to constantly be on your guard.

Dealing With an Absent Parent

Sometimes, protecting your children from overly-involved family members is the least of your worries. There are cases when people who should be involved in your children's lives are nowhere to be found. And you have the job of explaining to your children why their dad or mom doesn't come to see them.

"My ex was present at first," said Andi, "and now has vanished. We haven't heard from him in nearly two years. And he's dealing with some substance abuse issues. I tried to talk to the boys about it some. I don't want to constantly bring it up, but I want them to understand that their dad's issues are his issues, not theirs. They didn't cause it. They can't cure it."

"I think it's very important if there is an absent parent," explained Charles, "…that you do not allow the child to process that alone. You walk with them, with empathy, through the entire process. And let them ask whatever questions… because ultimately I believe you're teaching them how to relate to God in difficulty, and how to relate to God when things aren't happening according to what they feel should happen. So instead of trying to fix them, allow them to walk through the process."

Children aren't always capable of processing the pain and emotions they are experiencing on their own. As parents, it's our job to help them through any struggles or insecurities they may be having. The key is to know what damaging emotions our kids might be struggling with, and to recognize those times when they may need our help.

Children obey their parents. Adults honor their parents. Sometimes parents can use the previous authority that they had in your life to intrude in your relationship.

44

Healthy Boundaries With an Unhealthy Ex-Spouse

The dynamics change when you have an emotionally unhealthy ex-spouse who not only wants to be involved in their child's life, but tends to be over-involved.

Because of joint custody agreements, parents often have a legal obligation to share their children with someone who is not a good influence on their lives. Several of the successful stepfamilies we interviewed dealt with this problem, and their advice in this area was to set clear boundaries, and then articulate your expectations openly and regularly.

"We call meetings," said April. Any time a concern or issue would arise, she and Craig would address it head-on, no matter how uncomfortable it might be. And they made sure that both couples were present.

"I had to be direct and blunt on the phone," explained Daniel, "and [stress that] this is about the child. It's not about emotions and feelings."

When we compare ourselves to other people it is tormenting. Everybody looks good from a distance.

When it comes to our children, it's easy to allow tensions to run high and patience to run thin. But that's never the best way to handle an already uncomfortable situation. The key is to keep the focus on what's best for your children, and to continue reminding others to do the same.

Remember that children grow up, and there will be a time when issues of joint custody and shared living arrangements will no longer be a part of your life. But until then, face things head-on, with patience, diligence, and a lot of prayer.

Today's Reading

Ephesians 4:15; James 1:5; Romans 12:18

A Biblical Perspective

1) How would God have us respond to an ungodly or unbelieving ex-spouse?

2) What do these passages say about setting and communicating healthy boundaries with extended family members?

3) What are some other verses you know that address these types of difficult circumstances?

How We Blend

1) What are some of the most difficult extended family relationships you've had to navigate on the heels of your divorce or breakup?

2) Make a list of the people in your ex-spouse's family who still desire to play a role in your children's lives.

_____

_____

_____

_____

3) Of the relatives on this list, which ones would you consider a healthy influence on your children?

_____

_____

_____

4) Would you consider any of these relatives to be an unhealthy influence on their lives?

_____

_____

_____

5) How do you go about navigating your children's relationships with both of these groups of relatives?

6) The key to keeping kids safe from unhealthy people is to set clear and concise boundaries—both emotional and physical. What are some of the more effective boundaries you've set when it comes to your children?

7) How do you go about communicating and enforcing these boundaries?

8) Grandparents almost always want to play a role in their grandchildren's lives, no matter what circumstances arise. Discuss what role you see your ex's parents playing in your children's lives and future.

9) Do you consider your ex-spouse a healthy influence on your children? Why or why not?

10) What are some of the things they do that make you worry about your children when they are with your ex-spouse?

11) If you could ask them to change one particularly troublesome pattern of behavior around your children, what would it be?

12) Have you, or anyone in your group, ever had to deal with an absent ex-spouse? If so, discuss how you explained their absence to your children.

13) How did their absence affect your children? And how did you help them cope?

14) Read Psalm 27:10. What would this passage have to say to a child who is struggling to deal with an absent parent?

15) Close your group this week by praying for any children who may be struggling with an absent parent or an unhealthy extended family relationship.

For Personal Reflection

In the space below, write out how you plan to navigate difficult and unhealthy family relationships in the future. If these desires include setting new boundaries, explain how you plan to articulate and enforce these new boundaries. Then commit this week to pray for strength, wisdom, and resolve as you put these plans in motion.

_____

_____

_____

Between You And God

Heavenly Father, thank You for the promise of being near to all who call on You in truth, and for the promise of wisdom for those who ask. We are at times overwhelmed with the dynamics of family relationships regarding our precious children. We acknowledge You as the always-present, perfect Father, and ask that this reality would permeate our lives and the lives of our children. Protect them from harm, and lead them in the paths of righteousness. In Jesus' Name, Amen.

Session Eight
Special Blended Family Challenges

Most blended couples agree that life would be much easier if the courts were not so intimately involved in their lives or finances. But that's simply not the case for most stepfamilies, especially when the kids are young. Parents have an obligation to care for their kids, even after they divorce, and sometimes the state has to step in to make sure they do so. It's a necessity of life, but a breeding ground for conflict and resentment—especially among couples who are already struggling to get along.

Child Support Challenges

"Child support was a huge source of fighting with my ex-husband over the years," said Wanda. "It was always the threat of, 'I'm going to take it away from you somehow. I'm either going to take our daughter away from you so I don't have to pay child support… or I'll make sure that I don't make any money so you don't get any child support.'"

Like a lot of ex-husbands, Wanda's ex resented the idea of having to support children that weren't living under his roof, and he did all he could to punish his ex-wife for expecting it of him.

In a perfect world, people would always take care of their financial obligations, and voluntarily take care of their children. But we don't live in a perfect world, so sometimes the best approach is to step up and be the adult, even when others refuse to do so.

"You've really got to take into consideration the effect on the kids anytime you go into court," said Scott, "regardless of their age."

"It isn't actually the money," Craig reminded us. "It's the emotional time you invest, where the focus should be on your marriage, on your children, and on your faith. These are the things we should be focused on."

How to Handle Lawsuits

One of the most frustrating by-products of divorce is that the courts suddenly become intimately involved in your affairs. And the more financial and relational ties you have, the more involved they seem to be.

It is never healthy or harmless for kids when their parents have to go to court on their behalf, but it's a necessary evil that many blended families have to deal with. People don't always own their responsibilities to their children, so the courts are often the only place to turn when dealing with problems of child support and shared custody.

"It's a sad situation," said Charles, "and it should be treated as such. It shouldn't be, 'Oh, we won.' Well, not really. It's about the child and you have to think about what's going on in the child's mind. So throughout the entire process, that's what was on our minds… Not to over-spiritualize it, but it took a lot of prayer to really understand and get the proper perspective on the situation."

It's impossible to go through a lawsuit without feeling some sort of stress on your marriage and family. No one gets through a legal battle completely unscathed. The key is to keep the strain from affecting your family any more than necessary, and that takes a great deal of patience and maturity.

Child support can be a huge source of fighting between you and an ex-spouse. Consider not just the money, but also the stress the legal process will put on your marriage and children.

Being Fair Financially With Stepchildren

Another financial issue that stepfamilies have to deal with is being fair and equitable with all of your children and stepchildren. Jealousy is already a common problem among stepsiblings, so it's important not to add to that tension. In any family, children are sensitive to issues of fairness and equality, but in blended families, kids tend to be even more tuned into it. When one child feels that another is being favored, it can create a lot of resentment and anger.

Richard and Sheri both brought children into their marriage, so issues of equity were important to them from the start. Not just financially, but emotionally.

"It's not about making it to where it has to be exactly equal," explained Sheri. "It's important to us that this is 'our' family, 'our' kids. They're not your kids or my kids, they're our children, and that's how we treat it—as if we gave birth to all of them and as if we've always been together."

Stepchildren are often hypersensitive to issues of fairness, but it can feel exhausting to have to keep track of every dime you spend on every child in order to make sure you're being completely fair. Kids have different needs, and some will inevitably cost more than others. What's important is to make sure they understand their value in the family, and that all of their needs are being met—physically, emotionally, and financially.

Family Traditions and Holidays

Family traditions are important to children, and great ways for parents to create a sense of unity and belonging within the family. But in blended families, you often have competing expectations regarding these traditions. One set of children may be used to celebrating Christmas at home, while the other set always went to Grandma's for the holidays. His kids may expect turkey and dressing for Thanksgiving dinner, while hers always looked forward to Italian food.

Blending these family traditions together to make everyone happy isn't always easy, and often the best approach is to start fresh, and create new family customs.

"I think it's okay in a blended family to make your own traditions," explained Sheri, "to come up with a new way of doing things. It's your family. You guys have to make it work... We just said, 'We are going to do things our way. We're going to try some new things.'"

Blending family traditions takes a lot of compromise and creativity. You have to be willing to think outside the box, and then convince your children to do the same.

"Blending is compromising," added Craig. "Blending is adapting to different situations, and they change all the time."

Dealing With an Empty Nest

In every family, there comes a time when children leave home and couples are left alone to navigate their relationship as a married couple. In blended marriages, however, it may be the first time since the couple met that they are able to relate to each other as just husband and wife, with no children in the picture.

This doesn't sound like a huge problem, but for couples in blended families, it can be something of a shock to the system. They've been parents for so long, and have spent so much time and energy learning to blend, that they never really had the luxury of just focusing entirely on each other.

"The key to success in empty nesting," said Monte, "…is to really remember the reason why you fell in love in the first place. There are stresses with the kids, and stresses with family members, and maybe you're getting older, so there are other responsibilities to go with that. But you have to be a team."

In any marriage, the key to staying in love for a lifetime is focusing on each other's needs above all other human relationships. Whether blended or not, your spouse should be the most important person in your world, and nothing but your relationship with God should take a higher priority.

If you do that, your empty nest years will feel anything but empty.

Learning to find middle ground is critical for your new marriage and your relationship with the children.

Widowed and Blended

Remarriage under any circumstance can be challenging, but when the death of a spouse is involved, it can take on an even greater level of trial and struggle.

Many may think that marrying a widow or widower would be easier than having an ex-spouse still in the picture, but there are issues at work that aren't always apparent on the surface. And when kids are involved, those issues can be overwhelming.

"With the loss of a spouse, there's more anxiety and grief than one realizes," explained Monte. "There's a residual impact… that you don't always fully realize… In our relationship, as we were married, sometimes that would exhibit itself over time. And we had to adjust to that."

Monte was a widower when he met and married Kathleen. And he had many fond memories of his first wife. Unlike many divorced couples, Monte had nothing but good to say about his deceased wife, and his first marriage was a strong and healthy one. His kids also had fond memories of their mother when Kathleen came into the picture.

"I knew about [his wife]," said Kathleen, "and as things would get heightened, or disgruntled, she became a saint. And so I felt like I was competing with a saint, because as time grew, she got nicer and nicer and nicer… I dealt with a lot of jealousy. It really is hard to compete with a dead person."

One of the most difficult aspects of being married to a widow or widower, is that the ex-spouse never quite goes away. They are always lingering somewhere in the memories of those they left behind. The key is to understand that your marriage is not a competition. And that just because your husband or wife is grieving a previous spouse, doesn't mean they love you any less. Your relationship is a separate entity, not an extension of their first marriage.

It is possible for grief and love to co-exist. Even though your spouse's grief is real, so is their love for you and your family.

Today's Reading

1 Timothy 5:8; Psalm 94:19-22; Proverbs 16:7

A Biblical Perspective

1) What does the Bible say about our responsibility as parents to provide for our children?

2) How would God have us respond to those who shirk their financial responsibilities?

3) How can these scriptures be a guide and comfort to us during child support disputes?

How We Blend

1) In this week's video, Will and Wanda shared their struggles with endless court battles over child support issues. Do you have a similar testimony? If so, would you be willing to share it with the group?

2) How did these court battles affect your home and family? And how did you work to keep them from causing undue stress?

3) Will and Wanda eventually released her ex-husband from his child support obligations. Do you think they did the right thing? Discuss why or why not.

4) Lawsuit challenges can be exhausting for a family, and tough on children. How do you go about keeping the stress from affecting your marriage and family?

5) What would you do differently in the way you handled your legal negotiations if you had to do it again?

6) It's important to be fair in the area of finances when raising children and stepchildren. What have you done to make sure none of your children feel slighted?

7) What is most important to children when it comes to being fair and equitable in a blended family?

8) When dealing with finances in a blended family, what is the best way to be fair and equitable to all your children?

9) Why is it so important to structure a clear and comprehensive will when you have a blended family?

10) What is your most memorable family vacation or holiday experience?

11) What made this experience so memorable?

12) What are some of the more challenging areas of compromise you've had to make when planning family events or traditions?

13) What are some other areas of compromise you've had to make to keep your family united and on-track?

14) If you, or anyone in your group, have already reached the empty nest years, share some of your greatest joys and struggles since the kids have left home.

15) What advice would you give to couples preparing for an empty nest?

16) If you, or anyone in your group, have experienced the loss of a spouse, would you be willing to share your story? What was the greatest challenge you had to overcome as you remarried?

For Personal Reflection

In the space below, write out the most important or encouraging lesson you've learned throughout the course of this study. How will this new revelation affect the way you relate to your spouse and children in the future? What do you sense God saying to you about creating a healthy future for your blended family?

_____

_____

_____

Between You And God

Heavenly Father, we praise and thank You for bringing us together as a family, and for Your guidance and provision as we go through life together. When confronted by challenges, we ask for strength to meet them in a way that honors You, and protects our family. Help us shine the light of Your love to everyone around us—now and throughout all the years of our lives. In Jesus' Name, Amen.

Suggestions for Leaders

Leading a Bible study can feel like a daunting experience, but it's actually not that difficult—especially if it's a discussion format study. This particular series is designed to be an interactive conversation, not a class lecture. When leading the group, begin by seeing yourself as more of a facilitator than a teacher.

Here are a few suggestions to get you started, and to help things go more smoothly:

Preparing the Lesson

1) Begin by praying that God would guide you as you prepare to facilitate the lesson.

2) Before each session, make sure you have answered all the questions thoroughly, just as you would if you were attending the group.

3) After answering all the questions, go back and earmark those questions that you hope will lead to the most helpful and engaging conversations. This will help you remember any important points you hope to discuss.

4) Whenever possible, make notes of a personal story or anecdote to share in order to keep the conversation flowing.

5) While preparing to facilitate, try to identify two or three "big ideas" from each session that you hope the group will take away from the lesson. Note those in the margins so that you can highlight those particular points.

6) Remember that these lessons are designed to comfortably fill a 60-90 minute discussion format, so if your class is shorter or longer than that, you may need to cut a few questions, or add a few of your own.

7) Once you've prepared the lesson, cover the study in prayer. Pray that God would lead your thoughts and heart as you facilitate the study, and pray individually for each person in the group. Ask God to speak specifically to each person in the class.

Leading the Group

1) Remember to start and end on time. Lessons that run too long can easily drift off course. So try to keep the class focused, and keep your eye on the clock.

2) At the beginning of each class, remind the members of your group that this is a discussion class, and encourage everyone to participate.

3) Don't be afraid of silence. Sometimes people need time to process their thoughts, and if you always chime in and rescue the class, some might be less likely to participate.

4) Avoid answering your own questions. If you don't get a response, try restating the question in a different way.

5) Encourage more than one answer to each question. Once someone has answered, you might say, "That's a good answer. What do the rest of you think?" or "Does anyone else have any thoughts?"

6) Whenever possible, encourage members to share their personal stories or testimonies.

7) Learn to recognize rabbit trails, and quickly head them off before they take the discussion off-topic.

8) Never cut someone off in mid-answer. If people feel that their comments aren't important, they will shut down and stop responding.

9) Always end your lessons in a time of prayer. It's nice to have members of the group pray instead of always doing it yourself.

Lesson Format

Included with each workbook are eight videos created specifically for this study. These videos include candid interviews with many of the eighteen successful stepfamilies who agreed to help with this project. It also includes additional comments and teaching from Jimmy Evans. Be sure to begin each class by watching the session's corresponding video lesson, as these teachings are integral to the study.

Each lesson in the series also begins with a few short excerpts from our book *Blending Families.* These excerpts introduce the central theme of the week's lesson. This section is designed to be read by each member during the previous week, but you might decide to begin each lesson by reading this section aloud (or designating someone in the group to read it), since these excerpts set up many of the questions to follow.

A good way to begin each week is to ask if anyone has any concluding thoughts or comments from the previous session. Be careful not to allow too much discussion at this point, since you don't want to get ahead of the lesson.

Today's Reading

This section includes a few Bible verses that correlate with some of the points in this week's lesson. We suggest that you have someone read these passages aloud at the beginning of each session, and then open in a word of prayer.

A Biblical Perspective

This section includes a few questions regarding this week's Bible verses. Spend a few minutes at the beginning of each study discussing these questions, since they are designed to bring a biblical perspective to the lesson. Encourage members to keep these passages in mind as you begin.

How We Blend

The questions in this section are designed to be answered by each member during the previous week, so you might begin by asking if everyone had time to do that. Members should still be able to benefit from the study, even if they haven't done their homework, but discussions will be much more engaging if everyone comes prepared. It might be a good idea to remind the group each week to do that if at all possible.

As the group leader, we suggest that you be the one to read these questions aloud, instead of having members of the group take turns reading them. This allows you to rephrase each question in your own words when needed.

Remember that some questions can be answered rather quickly, while others might take a little time to process. So don't be afraid to pace yourself, and allow each question to be thoroughly explored before moving forward.

When appropriate, allow the discussion to sidetrack a bit. If someone has a good thought or follow-up question, let the discussion flow that direction. Some rabbit trails might be worth following. Just be prepared to bring the discussion back on topic when the time comes.

For Personal Reflection

This last section is intended as a way to conclude your lesson. Read this section aloud, and then give everyone a few minutes to write their responses in the space provided. Before ending in prayer, ask if anyone has any specific thoughts or prayer requests they'd like to share with the group.

Remember to end each lesson encouraging members to pray during the coming week for wisdom and guidance as God continues to speak to them through the course of this study.

Made in the USA
Monee, IL
18 April 2023

32049595R00037